Calm the F Down Coloring Book

Martin Chuzzlewit

Calm the F Down Coloring Book: Adult Coloring Book: Stress Relieving Designs and Patterns

Color Test Page

Unicorns are real.
And they're assholes!

My boss is a fucking, complicated wolf!

This bitch took me a long time to complete.

If you're gonna ride my ass at least pull my hair.

Don't you see, I am busy relaxing?
Now get the fuck out of here.

Silence is golden.
duct tape is silver.

Hey you bumblefuck, get out of my garden! Now!

Find your patience before I lose mine.

I never forget a face, but in your case I'll be glad to make an exception. Bitch!

With all due respect, you are a fucking, stupid jerk!

You go girl! And don't come back.

Now who would have thought that a fucking camel can be damn interesting!

So you think owls are cute? Or Wise? Or beautiful? Nope. They're just nocturnal knobjockeys.

Always speak politely to an enraged dragon.

Float like a butterfly, sting like a bee.

Denial ain't just a river in Egypt.

Owls have nine lives. All of them are fucking miserable.

Good things come to those who bait.

What's the use of happiness?
It can't buy you money.

Don't take yourself so seriously, no one else does.

Tell me... Is being stupid a profession or are you just gifted?

Me? Sarcastic? Never.

I'll always cherish the original misconception I had of you.

Printed in Great Britain
by Amazon